The contents and creations herein are the property of their respective artist(s) and may not be used or reproduced without explicit written consent. The following works have been donated from prisoners across the United States and are published with permission in order to amplify the voices of queer and trans people surviving imprisonment.

A.B.O. Comix Collective is sustained by volunteers, community donations, grant funding, and various daring bank heists. We run on the perserverance, bravery, kindness, empathy, and love that our contributors share with us.

Edited by Ollie Mills
Cover Design by Casper Cendre
Cover Illustration by Horace Thomas

©A.B.O. Comix 2022

Table of Contents

About..4
Foreword..5

Part 1
a slave behind // These bars..6
   Michael Eaton | The Poet..7
   Jason Cooper | Static..8
   Pariah | Lying down and waking up a slave in Texas......9
   Tsunami | Coping With..11
   Anonymous | Scissors...12
   Sakura Ai | Torn...14
   Michael Eaton | Darkness...15

Part 2
Love may bloom again from a seed..................................16
   Summer Breeze | A Convict's Love Song......................17
   Horace Thomas | To You..18
   Scary Movie | Untitled..19
   Mark Lott | Let Me Know You...20
   H. Lee | Love...21

Part 3
filling one another with fullness..22
   Billy D. Thomas | Bad Boys' Hearts................................23
   Billy D. Thomas | popping trunk.....................................24
   Billy D. Thomas | in i first Came a Joy............................25
   Jesse Dubois | Untitled..26
   M. Ramsey-El | Butterfly...29

Part 4
it was time to return home // and hide from death............31
   Max Wolf | Rain...32
   Horace Thomas | Memories...33
   Fuller | Little Scraps of Paper...34

Ch4per Rise | 'Tis the Night..35
H. Lee | Oreo!..36
Bree Bree | Dreaming..38
Fuller | four flowers..39

Part 5
no silhouette if there's never a sun..................................40
Horace Thomas | God's Eyes..41
Mecca | Amen..42
Fuller | To say goodbye to maybe......................................45
Mark Lott | Life of Time...46
James David West, Jr. | Drive Carefully.............................47
Trouble "The Goat"| A Mother's Love................................48
Lil Cee Cee | Regret Forces Reflections............................49
Scary Movie | Again...50
Mr. Patrick G. Burton | "A Changed Man".........................52
Mark Lott | Strife...53

Part 6
Chew them up // Spit them out // Repeat........................54
Marsh | Culture is a Communicable Infectious Disease Pt. 1.....55
Michael Eaton | Time Machine...56
Shon Pernice | Who I Am...58
Marsh | Culture is a Communicable Infectious Disease Pt. 2.....59
Billy D. Thomas | Mending The Broken.............................60
H.Lee | Our World..61
Mark Lott | A World That's Free...62
Scary Movie | Hourglass..63

Afterword..64
How To Help..65

3

About

A.B.O. Comix is a collective of creators and activists who work to amplify the voices of LGBTQ prisoners through art. By working closely with prison abolitionist and queer advocacy organizations, we aim to keep queer prisoners connected to outside community and help them in the fight toward liberation. The profits we generate go back to incarcerated artists, especially those with little to no resources. Using the DIY ideology of "punk-zine" culture, A.B.O. Comix was formed with the philosophy of mutual support, community, and friendship.

Our collective is working towards compassionate accountability without relying on the state or its sycophants. A.B.O. Comix believes our interpersonal and societal issues can be solved without locking people in cages. Our mission is to combat the culture that treats humans as disposable and disproportionately criminalizes the most marginalized amongst us. Through artistic activism, we hope to proliferate the idea that a better world means redefining our concepts of justice.

Find us online at www.abocomix.com

With love and solidarity,
A.B.O. Comix Collective

Foreword

peace
    in a world without walls
    extends beyond the inner,
    becomes collective power.

  words
      resisting walls
      are radiant, rageful, peaceful,
      prayerful.

      in the after-rage,
      committed words are:
      family
      comradeship
      church.

            (under song,
            crumbling on windowsills,
            tucked in elders' books,
            nested
            in letters
            upon letters
            fear and love and loss of faith,
            dysphoria, regret and
            insurgent queer joy
            rattle in defiance of death
            and chains.)

    we generate
    an after-walls
    world with our
    courage to write,
    share, ignite, burn.

                          - *Ollie Mills*

Part 1

a slave behind // These bars

Michael Eaton | The Poet

Love comes

Stinging upon razor's edge
Two hearts contorted to will
Urged beyond moral boundary

Liberated
              from the laceration of post

Pristine anguish
              wrapped in tranquil embrace.

Now revised
Assurance lost
Hindered by proxy

        Only black letters
                    immersed
                              in a sea of white.

Jason Cooper | Static

When the world's drear and drab
and we can not cohab--
itate with those we love
on earth, or above
where can solace be found
in noise that goes around
our head but not our heart
distraction is a start
yet I can not be full
when I'm made static's fool.

Pariah | Lying down and waking up a slave in Texas

It's poetic...

IN TEXAS, we're trapped in pits with small windows.

Inside these cells, we're funding our own imprisonment; the chains are encrypted inside the chips and soup sales.

We're inside of an identity crisis believing our soul's out of Favors,

So we accept the chains;
believing a greater change will come save us...

"Can you dig that?!?!"

I guess the Willie Lynch syndrome dies hard in some places.

Since I'm older now...

IN THESE YOUNGER GUYS, I see my own reflection.

It seems as if the hate for ourselves is baked in.
Perhaps it takes breaking one down,
In order to build one up and to make a man.

I used to beat up on myself!

The whipping took away my strength...
Then I killed my bad habits and drug 'em to a ditch!

I changed from a threat to a
Promise;
but in Texas I'll always be a number.

Everyday it's the same old song...

In doubt: our systematic-scars Found a home.
In Texas: it's death before parole.
In Unity: We can overcome!

But we won't...

Because by the throat we're holding our resolve under the water.

Christians and Muslims accept this torture.

The trauma cemented the bangers in a corner;
self-tripping, cooking drink and getting stoned.

I envision us standing up for ourselves,
and not being exploited with little to no health care.

But tomorrow we'll be back in the

"Fields"

Under a sun giving off heat like hell!

There ain't a Night
I don't look beyond these walls with cataract
Eyes, and pull in the stars.

Today's a blessing...

Every good one, I'll record them.

Tomorrow I'll wake up a slave behind these
These bars.

Tsunami | Coping With...

The days pass by, on my cot I lay
Cry out to me creator as I bow to pray.

Help me through a difficult season!

I don't always understand, but know
All things have a reason.

Some days are harder than the
Rest, my faith and patience put to the
Test

Loved ones die while I'm far away
I cry again as I bow to pray.

In the midst of despair, there are blessings
Here, and Bertie, my friend, always
Reminds me she is near.

Through pen and paper we forged a
Friendship, we have now time tested
True kinship.

Let this be an example to those who need
To know, you can find strength and
Support from someone you may not yet
Know.

My experiences have helped me to love others
With a love that's true. The ones full of
Hurt, who need me and you.

Anonymous | Scissors

I'd like to take some scissors to my face
Disgusted with the sight of the place
Lips spread to lie, teeth grin and I
Take pleasure in the pain brought to life

I'd like to take some scissors to my chest
Terrified by my cold-hearted test
Allowed the lie to come alive
Pushed it to prosper, nurtured to strive

I wish I could turn back time
Undo this lie, unhurt your eyes
To what I'm capable of
My propensity

Are you sorry
Are you sorry you ever loved me?

I'd like to take some scissors to my chin
Mutilate the face that holds this grin
My tongue's a flame I never tamed
Agonizing source of total shame

I'd like to take some scissors to my brain
Horrified by the depth of this pain
Sever the shit - I'm part of it
And my worthlessness is definite

You tried and you tried
Your best was undermined
The choice was my choice
And I ignored your voice

Reason cries out
Reason snuffed out
Scissors to me
Scissors clipping
Scissors to me
Guilty, dripping

With sweat as I run
Run from the gun
Like escaping the sun
It never lasts
The past is never passed
It always lasts
The past always lasts

Are you sorry
Are you sorry you ever loved me?

Sakura Ai | Torn

I hate this world if it exists
People are all fake dying in piss
All their hatred for to make me feel
What's the meaning of their faith, is it real

Enjoy the suffering I tend to be
Hearing you talk as they hate me
What must I trust even if you lie
To my face, behind my back - say bye

I walk away. Is this how you pull me in
As I stand by myself left in pity no win
Then what, I'm invisible to all once here
Like a nightmare, my dreams erased in air

Is there a leader to end hatred of people
Or am I always alone, not once equal
But I feel alone, only the voice who guides
He is me or she but I have to choose to abide

Who am I? A sad tale never been born
I'm emotionally believing my life, my heart - torn!

Like a piece of paper I write my concern
My world, my faith, their hatred please all leave - burn!

None other less, no mercy for them 'cause they hate me.

Michael Eaton | Darkness

The Dark is generous...

Its first gift
   is concealment: our true faces lie in the dark beneath our skins, our true hearts remain shadowed deeper still.

But the greatest concealment lies not in protecting our secret truths, but in hiding from us the truths of others.

The dark protects us from what we dare not know...

Its second gift
   is comforting illusion: the ease of gentle dreams in night's embrace, the beauty that imagination brings to what would repel day's harsh light.

But the greatest of its comforts is the illusion that the dark is temporary.

Day is the illusion.

Its third gift
   is the light itself: as days are defined by nights that divide them, as stars are defined by the infinite black through which they wheel, the dark embraces the light, and brings it forth from the center of its ownself.

With each victory of the light it is the darkness that wins.

The darkness is generous, and it is patience, and it always wins.

But in the heart of its strength lies weakness: one lone candle is enough to hold it back.

Love is more than a candle...

        Love, it can ignite the stars.

Part 2

Love may bloom again from a seed

Summer Breeze | A Convict's Love Song

Co-nv-ic-ts

This poem goes out to all my convicts
I got love for all my convicts!

Police got you locked up in jail
Your friends and family can't make your bail

Your dusty foot celly stinking up the cell
It feels like your life is a living hell

To all my convicts in this struggle
Stay strong till the End

Keep the faith and you'll win
Remember...
What don't kill you, can only make
you stronger

My convicts!

Co-nv-ic-ts

This poem goes out to all my convicts
I got love for all my convicts.

Horace Thomas | To You

I look at you like family
Though we're a world apart
Concrete walls and bars
Doesn't stop our start...

To wade through the water
Or the burning pit of hell
We'll get through this
And somehow prevail...

When I look out my window
I see mountains and hills
Tell me what you think
How you feel?

Let's always stay in touch
And this way we will know
The path we are traveling
Emotions that we sow!

When we rise in the morning
Let's put another layer
Sealing our friendship
With a prayer!

Scary Movie | Untitled

A riddle wrapped in a mystery
That would put Mister Hitchcock to shame
Untold worlds within a galaxy
George Lucas couldn't even explain

Layer upon layer of intrigue
Leaves my heart at the edge of its seat
There's so much suspense in your eyes
That I gave up reading Tom Clancy

There is a depth inside of you girl.
A hundred lifetimes could not explore
But it wouldn't keep me from trying
To unveil all the things I adore.

Mark Lott | Let Me Know You

The one thing I'd love nothing more to do,
Is for you to let me know you.
From the inner beauty deep inside,
Or even those secrets you most want to hide.
How to love you and make you mine,
and even care for you down the line.
To let me know how to be a friend,
In which to forever by you stand.
To teach me things I'd never know,
or show me steps in which to grow.
To overcome adversity each day,
To forever find my own way.
A person to count on when down and blue,
So please let me know you.

H. Lee | Love

Love is so much like a flower
Beginning like a weed
Growing out of nowhere
From the tiniest seed
Love grows slowly
Like a bud upon a stem
Not sure yet what it wants
Forming a feeling - a shape within
Love taking shape
Suddenly it's in full bloom
Bursting forth in all its glory
A sweet fragrance that fills a room
How long it lasts
Varies with its care
Nurtured it goes on
Neglected it shows despair
Flowers so much like love
Petals and feeling wither then die
The loss of such beauty
'Tis reason to sigh
Yet, love lost, is beauty no more
Becomes once again a weed
Starting over the cycle
Love may bloom again from a seed

Part 3

filling one another with fullness

Billy D. Thomas | Bad Boys' Hearts

Bad boys' hearts, we love through our pain

To help overcome our past shames, forgiving the ones who broke into me

The one that scarred me inside out.

Bad boys' hearts, the scars remain

As the pain parts, my love-filled heart cries out for embrace

One to hold, someone to understand.

Bad boys' hearts, I pour out my love

To overcome my heart, at times I love to be the one wearing the shirt

Covered in our heart-spurts.

Bad boys' hearts, lovers: we need someone to love & hold

Someone to embrace, filling one another with fullness

And the love

Bad boys' hearts need.

Billy D. Thomas | popping trunk -

- then down-casting me for liking you. There,

"isn't that the pot calling the kettle black? who Do You Think You Are by judging me for the jacket
You also Wore in the closet?

"it's my Life, my Time and my Trunk being popped and filled with Junk that overFlowed from Your past.

"so You Judging me openly For What You Do in Darkness. It will come To The Light."

I Was Yet The YouthFul Boy
You came and took for Your own selfish Joys.

You Broke me Down and Tore me inside out,
Drugging and Altering my state of mind only so later on You can point Your finger at me to keep the others off YourSelf.

If only you knew then that All Things put Together in The Dark Will also be Brought To The Light.

The judgement You pinned on me and The prison You Had me bound up in, You will also open Your eye To Find Your self Back in To Them.

You That Do Then Judge are The ones soon To Face Your own Judgement, for That Block of Stumbling You Put Before me as a YouthFul Boy.

Then It Will Be I who God sets Free.

Giving Back To You The same crap You put into me.

So You Judges are Law makers That cast me Down and out Bound in this mental state

O GOD I am here and I wait.

Billy D. Thomas | in i first Came a Joy
Time came and went JoyFul

Time I well Spent;
Broken and Long Time over-used
Now warped And out of Tune.

OLD and DeFlowered, now I am Cast
Out of sight and out of mind;
      Now come the new to be used.

Still and over-gripped, too tight to
      Slip. Haters take the stand;
      New lies They now Tell.

Off in The Shadows I hear and see
The evil Deeds You First Did To I,

Broken, Yes, Yet Feelings Have I.

With Wisdom Pain I Of Past I
Do ReCall, These Cell Bars I'll
OverCome Yet. You in I, The
Pain of Wisdom is here To Stay.

Old But Wisdom I have and I
Pray I'll still be played...

Jesse Dubois | Untitled

I found a love that I cannot shake
One that keeps my heart awake

I know one day I'll have to go
I can't handle it, the pain will show

I don't understand this feeling I feel
But I know it is so real

It pokes and prods at my soul
Awakening my heart of coal

As it ignites the embers within
Love, how do I start? Where to begin?

I am scared to go away
My heart it hurts this very day

I love one love, oh, how sweet!
This one is the person I wanted to meet

Now that I have I'm not ready to go
These tears, my love, I know they'll show

There once was a man who drove me crazy
Without him around I felt extremely hazy

Lost in my body and soul I may be
And without his love I cannot see

Can't see into the aspiration that lies ahead
Everything around me starts feeling so dead

I sliver into the realm of all my personal emotion
Lost with no quiver or bow, walking in slow motion

Seeing the emotions run through my body like my blood,
Beating inside my heart like a flood

I don't get the feeling of rage inside
Or the feeling of love I need to satisfy my pride

To fill this hole in my soul and heart
That had driven me from the start

So can I just have this man's love?
I say this prayer to the spirits above:

Let my life steadily progress through this change
So I don't have to be like a dog with mange

So turn the page, open the door and let him in
Because with him, I know I can win

Here I am in a world so cold
Am I a man that is so bold?

As the ice breaks beneath my feet
I tend to want to sit down in my seat

As the world falls apart around me
I know all it takes is one to see

That the world can be better
All of it starts with one big letter

That letter is one so unknown
It takes one to change the world.

The unknown letter is I.
You may sit and ask why

Look up into the sky above!
See into your heart, love

Look into a Mirror and see yourself
Learn the things you love and put them on a shelf

A smile so big no matter how ugly that may seem
It carries one thing, and that's your own gleam

You and you alone brightens the world around
the letter I is the one that makes things sound

As I wake to see the full moon
it reminds me that I'm out soon

I cannot wait for this day to come
When I walk out I know I'm done

I know when I go home that I am free
When that time comes I can just be me

I am a man who is nice at heart
One who loves every day since the start

I'll finally have a chance to open up
When I walk out I'll have a full cup

Right now my glass is only half full
I walk away from here to turn into a jewel

One that alone brightens the room
And brings everyone joy, not doom

I will be a man who is not just great
But one who doesn't have to scream in debate

So I still await the day that I leave this prison
This time I will make a better decision

I'll stay away from these gates
The ones that drive me irate

So please, cruel prison, let me go
So I can be the one to the world know

That if I can change, they can too
I am whole, I am brand new

On my way out I will smile
'Cause every smile is worthwhile.

M. Ramsey-El | Butterfly

Hello my little Butterfly,
I just wanted to say hi.
To have my voice vibe to you on the inside
Where you hide behind
Your silk coccoon, wrapped warmly in your private room.

Soon you will be free, and I can't wait, but for now...

Rest your head, my little Butterfly.
Just allow my words to kiss you gently on your thoughts
As you dream the Perfect dream of angels' wings.
See Heaven as you sleep and keep soft clouds
Beneath your feet.

In a wink you will be free, and I can't wait, but for now...

Rest your head, my little Butterfly.
Know that I will always be by your side.
I will be here for all your cares. I will protect you from every
Nightmare. For whatever makes your tender heart sacred,
I will be there.

In mere days you will be free, and I can't wait, but for now...

Rest your head, my little Butterfly.
Know that you are already loved.
Feel my warm hands cover you. With these hands I will
Forever hug you. With these hands I will never let you go.
With these hands I will hold you always.

One day you will be free, and I can't wait, but for now...

Rest your head, my little Butterfly.
Know that you are so beautiful.
Know that you will have the Sun and Moon.
Know that because of you the stars will move. You will
create wonders undiscovered with your colorful thoughts.
Know that there will be no reason to cry.
No sadness will water your eye.

Know that joy will be in your life.
That there will always be light.
That you will always shine because
God has made you forever bright...

But for now, just rest your head, my little Butterfly.

It's not yet time to rise.
And know that when you do finally open your eyes
I hope you recognize my voice and smile,
Knowing that I have made you wings to fly.

Part 4

*it was time to return home //
and hide from death*

Max Wolf | Rain

Rain, rain coming down like big drops of liquid rainbows.

I smell the rain coming from the west,

Before it starts to come down for the glory of the Heavens.

I sit under this maple tree listening to the drops of the rain.

It's playing musical tones on the wind waves of this big loving heart of mine.

I see a lady off in the distance, dancing rhythmically to the falling of the rain, rain.

I see her jump up like a reversed liquid raindrop.

I see a mourning dove fly away into a rainbow.

Horace Thomas | Memories

I miss standing on the corner
While the sky pours rain
The smell of fresh air
Water flowing down the drain...

The sound of rain drops
Falling on the ground
It's something magical
Listening to its sound...

The sky is beautiful
The clouds are near
Life is that moment
We all revere...

Every moment of life
Can sometimes be a spectacle
The mind with memories
Like a receptacle...

Fuller | Little Scraps of Paper

   I found these little scraps of paper
tucked inside my mamaw's bible
   There were pictures of us kids
when we was missing our front teeth
   And every time I think about her
I just smile and say my prayers
   'Cause you were watching over me
when I was running in the street
   Now there's contracts, bills, and deadlines
just sign here if you please.
   All the stress of this insanity
nearly knocks me to my knees.
   Our lives just little scraps of paper
and all we ever want is more
   But I'd give anything to go back
and walk right through that door
   To have her tell another story
about their lives way back when
   Her eyes would sparkle when she laughed
and then she'd smile that big ol' grin
   She'd show me little scraps of paper
about her cousin so and so

   Why do we always want to hurry?
And do we really gotta go?

   It's just a little scrap of paper
but I wrote it from the heart
   Every day I write another one
even though I ain't too smart

Ch4per Rise | 'Tis the Night

'Tis the night before my incarceration;
When alien invasions got kids tripping
Over radio stations, when trumped
up administrations got people's
Brainwaves fading; you're being
Chased by Jasons at voting stations
Or being tricked off by chicks in cheetah
Prints masquerading. Is it the Cuts
For your luck or your eyes wide shut
As the devil laughs in front of the
Class, playing the mandolin, skins
Are turning to cancer from the wicked
Winds, contorting and screwing the
Unseen hand; seeing what mankind's

doing.

Evil men are processing rockets
Blowing up mountains, poisoning
Children's water fountains, and uncle
Sam's wicked hands are scratching
The turn tables, while old ladies
Break dance to old men's fables
Since Cain and Abel this world
Has been unstable; the Constitution's
On drugs so justice has got a bad
Label, Trump is slicker than
Clark Gable.

A pit and a pendulum; through the
Devil's Navel; passing our
Energies MK-ultra, the government's
Reverse psychologies, sinister enemies
Using Modern Day Slavery, Am I
Vested in this country, or is it
Vested in Me; double breasted
Technologies paid in degrees;
Answering Questions, of no-one
Praying to God on their knees

From <u>eons</u> to <u>eons</u> my thoughts
Far and Beyond, we don't even
Have <u>preachers</u> to <u>trust.</u> Is it ashes
To <u>Ashes</u> or is it <u>Dust</u> to <u>Dust</u>?
Instead of teaching the knowledge
They want to keep
On <u>touching us.</u>

Son of <u>Adam</u>

Who can be the last one <u>remaining</u>
<u>Hydroplaning</u>; through generations
And die in <u>vain</u> using in vitro
<u>Fertilizations</u> and still nothing's
Changing, <u>Carbon Copies</u> of the same
Thing; yet I keep striving, more
Alive than an <u>85iver; digital</u>
Thinking; brain waves, an illuminating
Live wire; once you inspire & explore
Your <u>heart's desires</u> you can breathe
Fire <u>leaving your seeds to reach higher!</u>

H. Lee | Oreo!

Oreo! Oreo!
Wherefore art thou, Oreo?

Where is it you bide
Your time when you hide?
Where do you lie
While the world you espy?
In your garden, do you wait
Using birds for bait?
Ready to chase a few
To add to your menu?
You do as you please
Lying in the A/C breeze
Lookin' so cool
Upon the stool you rule
Are you so poised and debonair?
On the shelf, that's your lair
Dozing away without a care
With dust motes dotting your hair
Is that you on the window sill,
Watching the people for a thrill?
Wanting to chase each and every one
Catching none; it's all for fun
Searching high, searching low
Only you know where you go

Oreo! Oreo!
Wherefore art thou, Oreo?!

Bree Bree | Dreaming

I must be dreaming
      golden roads
           golden gates
                  fast cars and flashy toes!

                        dreaming is my Reality
                                it's destiny
                  yellow Purple blue Ribbons

        Love sparking the air
        Pleasant dreaming!
        A house well-built
        candles blowing!

            Music
            Flowing
        Softly Dreaming.

Fuller | four flowers

halfway around the world
        in the swirling muddy water
of a long-forgotten polluted river
        four flowers
floated by on their way to the sea

children played under the stars
        as the people danced
                by light from the fires

the bodies burned long into the night
        when the sun began to rise in the sky
            they all left that place
                and searched for food

then it was time to return home
        and hide from death

Part 3

no silhouette if there's never a sun

Horace Thomas | God's Eyes

They shut down the yard today
While on the ground dead
Prisoners lay...
The smell of gas still lingers in
The air, it's in your hair, it's
Everywhere. A scent you're
Forced to bear...You can
Feel the Tension. Not to
Mention the hostility. All
Around...As we observe
Without a word the blood
Sucked up by the ground...
We've grown to learn
That soon they will return
Regardless of your
Participation we all must
Face this harsh disgrace
And this unfair situation...
Tonight some loved one will shed
A tear once they realize their
Greatest fear. A sad penalty they
Must pay when told how their
Loved one was dragged away...
The thought of their loved one
Who died in vain, their precious
Blood running down the drain...
The underlying reason will never
be told, why the Reaper came
To claim another soul.
We all have faltered and
Stumbled along the way,
Mine decades ago, others'
this very day...If one is
Capable of holding on, be
assured it won't be long;
People will soon realize
It's all being recorded in
God's eyes.

Mecca | Amen

I
Only god can judge me
Fuck a judge & jury.
I fell in love w/ selling drugs for
Franklins, Grants & jewelry.
You understand my story, well I
mean you planned it for me.
How am I wrong for who I am?
Can't understand it. Surely
There's a mistake that's being made;
you plan to punish who?
These declarations have me thinking
something's wrong w/ you.
You made the world & all that's in it;
this fuck-up is on you.
How can you blame me for surviving?
Who the fuck is you?
I'm not ungrateful or rude, I'm
simply something new.
Ain't nobody ever give me shit, who
was coming though.
Sleeping in them halls, my hoodie on,
not knowing what to do,
My parents weren't around, I was
scared, where the fuck was you?

II
I started sellin' crack & snortin'
dawg at the same time.
I killed my closest friend, it doesn't
hurt, you & I know why.
Sunday I can't go to church, time
is money, Krazy huh?
But you already knew how things
would go from day one.

Aren't you the one who made the
world in 7 business days?

Murderers & rapists they've been here
since the beginning days,
Aren't you the one who told the
world what we should sit & praise –
so why is it you give us crime, why
is it you give us AIDS?
Why is it we lack the opportunities
to get away from bigots that you put in place?
It's obvious I understand so little of your plans,
All I'm asking is a glance, just a
glimpse of where we stand.
Amen...

V
Since only you can judge me,
Fuck you & your criticisms.
For me, this life is Fitting; damn
whoever deems me sinner.
I don't entertain your mirror, I will
not retain your image.
Sodom & Gomorrah, Stonewall - just
to name a few.
Clad in the flesh again, last to impress
upon the world an ideology
where nothing is correct in it...
You're the one that stressed **rigid**,
never gave us rest, winded.
Hitler was one of your tests.
Trump, is he one too?
Sitting wherever you sit, laughing,
It's funny as shit.
Ostracizing anyone who tells you
your methods are sick.
But I don't want to change you, all
I ask is compromise.
You can rule in heaven, give me
hell and I'll be fine!

VI
Aren't you the one who made the
world in 7 business days?

I wish you'd rewind it, maybe try
this shit a different way.
Aren't you the one who told the world
about religious praise?
Why the fuck you give us Trump, why
you think this shit's a game?!
Why is it I had to do eleven, wasn't
there a way —
to set me free & live up to my name.
Show me a different way.
It's obvious I understand so little
of your plans.
I'm through praying for a glance, a
glimpse of where we stand.
Amen...

Fuller | To say goodbye to maybe

To say goodbye to maybe
To shed a tear for why
I can't give up on crazy
I refuse to even try

So return to me in silence
Your thoughts I've always shared
I go again into that place
Where once we used to care

Avarice meanders slowly
Capricious in its lust
I'm lost again in folly
Searching for that misplaced trust

If I ever get to handle
Something precious as before
I'll try hard to respect it
And to cherish all the more

So venture once again with me
That thought to which I cloy
I'll never be apart from you
My hope, my peace, my joy

Mark Lott | Life of Time

Some people ask how can it be
I grew up like I did and can still be me.

To be bullied, beaten, molested, and taught wrong,
Yet still find a way to overcome and stay strong.

Little do they know how hard it is,
To live daily and have to think of this.

And try as I might to forgive and forget,
It's hard not to relive the torment.

If people only knew the things it may cause,
They would understand the reason I have flaws.

To search each day for someone in which to confide,
While learning to stay in stride.

To be abandoned, rejected, hurt and judged too.
All the while I set out to prove,

That I know what it is like to live a life like mine,
While trying to live a life of time.

James David West, Jr. | Drive Carefully

Two thoughtless fellows had cars they thought perfection;
They met one day at an intersection.
Tooted their horns and made a connection.
A police car came and made an inspection;
An ambulance came and made a collection.
All that is left is recollection
With two less votes in the next election.
And two graves more in a cemetery section.

Trouble "The Goat" | A Mother's Love
dedicated to Jeanna Ballard, "My Queen"

4 walls surround me
Just a ceiling and the floor
And a slab of concrete

A spit sink and toilet made from stainless steel:
No way I thought that I'd ever see myself live

A mat laid by a mind full of agony;
Nothing in this jail cell could ever be of pleasuring

My mind is overrun by so many apologies,
One to the memory of a wonderful mother
who acknowledges me!

Drugs and that paper took me in at 13.
When will I redeem? When will I be seen?
When do I replenish to a better life of dreams?
When will I be free again?

And while I walk around this world like I'm still
A true thug,
I soon drop a tear
Since I've lost a mother's love

Now with all the anger inside of me,
I need a mother's touch.
But too doomed to ask, after all the s**t that
I've done, done.

So now, what does that make me? A stupid mother's
F**k up
Why, because the things I've done could
Never be recovered?

Yeah, I did things wrong but doesn't mean that I
Ain't love her
And I'll do <u>anything</u> to have my mother's love back again!

Lil Cee Cee | Regret Forces Reflections

alone in this world, with so many people,

yet no one seems to understand me alone in this world,

even
        myself, for I've yet to "fully" understand me.

alone in this world, no shadow to lead,

no silhouette if there's never a sun,

alone in this world, so I pray for the light

to guide me when darkness comes.

Scary Movie | Again

Even after all this time
I can still picture your tears
Running down your pretty face
Heartbreaking and crystal clear
I can still feel your last touch
Your phantom arms around me
And still feel your chest heaving
As I held you close to me
Your sad beautiful eyes
Releasing all your anguish
My shirt soaked with all your tears
Your face pressed against my chest

If I could relieve your pain
Do all that I could to take
Away all your misery
Just so those tears don't streak
Down that lovely face of yours
I would do that and much more
So those tears don't ever stain
That sweet little heart of yours

Again

If there was a way
To turn back the hands of time
I'd take back all the pain I've caused
With those hurtful words of mine
I'd take you in my arms
Look right into your eyes
With heartfelt sincerity
Baby I'd apologize
I'd wake up every morning
Kiss you lightly on your brow
Tell you how much I love you
That we'll make it through somehow

*If I could relieve your pain
Do all that I could to take
Away all your misery
Just so those tears don't streak
Down that lovely face of yours
I would do that and much more
So those tears don't ever stain
That sweet little heart of yours*

Again

If there's a way to give you
A life filled with happiness
I'd walk through the halls of hell
To ensure you'd get the best
I'd do whatever it takes
Just to show you my true heart
That what I feel inside
Isn't just a façade
I only want you to know
For you I'd do anything
To prove that the love I have
Is more than what it seems

*If I could relieve your pain
Do all that I could to take
Away all your misery
Just so those tears don't streak
Down that lovely face of yours
I would do that and much more
So those tears don't ever stain
That sweet little heart of yours*

Again

Mr. Patrick G. Burton | "A Changed Man"

"A Changed Man" is who I am
And will continue to be
Not only for myself,
But for my entire family.
Because I've caused enough pain,
Some that won't go away,
I'm truly regretful and working on
Being better every day.

It will be a process
That I'll never give up on,
If I mess up again,
My loved ones will be gone.
I can't risk losing them,
I'm going to let them see
That I'm a good person
And please don't doubt me.

Because "All Things Are Possible,"
If only you believe and try
God's given me another chance,
I refuse to let it pass me by.

I'm going to take advantage of it,
By walking a straight line:
Nothing's going to stop me
From doing what's right this time.

Of course I'm not perfect,
None of us are,
But we are all capable of excelling
And going very far.
And I'm going to do
Whatever I possibly can,
To prove to everyone, including myself,
That I am...

        "A Changed Man"

Mark Lott | Strife

How can one say he knows what it's like,
To live a life full of strife.

Where as a small boy you are abused,
Which causes you to be confused.

The hurt it introduces to one's life,
Is like constantly being stabbed with a knife.

Hurt, betrayed and confused,
Those things in life you start to do,

As a learned behavior from the past,
You wear it around like a cast.

No positive do you know,
You stay in denial as you grow.

Then you start to blame yourself,
And know of no help,

The one day out of the blue,
It finally hits you.

That of all things in this life,
You have learned to live in strife.

Part 6

Chew them up // Spit them out // Repeat

Marsh | Culture is a Communicable Infectious Disease, Pt. 2

What would you do if you could do...
Anything.

What would you become if you were...
Disconnected.

A manifestation of infecting memes
Artificial fibers soaking up stains

Colors change
Something strange left in its place

What would you do if your world collapsed
If you woke up in a cage

If your self-hate awoke in a rage
If your family was on the front page

If the world was a stage
Upon which everyone spoke lies

Read your role in real time
Straight from the script

Execute perfectly this chaotic jumble
What happens next?

What would you do if your better angel
Killed itself

What would you do if your better angel
Stamped out its competition

Left a beautiful soul destroyed
He was only a boy...

What would you do?

Michael Eaton | Time Machine

Buried within Humanity's Failures

Leaving Behind

                                              Those we love,

                            forced to live under

                                      false rule.

To live under the lies of those sworn to protect

                                            Those we love.

The Powerful

                fault the unfortunate with

                                  ease.

Destroying families with guilt

                guilt of their own failures

                      Who's really guilty?

Those who promote positive behavior

                        Through

                              Tyranny and

                                              Repression?

The.

Real.

Criminals.

They destroy man's natural existence, leaving us

Broken

Helpless

Damned.

Return to the machine of their making

                                                          Chew them up

                                                          Spit them out

                                                          Repeat.

Shon Pernice | Who I Am

I may be your neighbor,
Or work as a caterer.
I might serve your food,
Or fix your hairdo.
I am a taxpayer,
And may be a bricklayer.

There are some occupations,
That reject my persuasions.
A job application,
Comes with consternation.
Mention a background check,
My heart hits the deck.

All that I ask,
Is to give me a chance.
My mistakes of the past,
They were treated with an iron cast.
Time has given me skills,
And has strengthened my will.

I will prove my worth,
As I embark on new turf.
I feel like an outcast;
How long will this last?

As I live in your community,
I yearn for the unity.
What you see is the real me,
Living with a felony.

Marsh | Culture is a Communicable Infectious Disease, Pt. 3

The mother of invention, Necessity

Prison for a teen:
A lesson in Necessity

You learn to hide in plain view
Shave your head, become a tattoo
To be whatever it is you have to be
In order to make it through

Occasionally you see an example
Of whom you see yourself to be
And wonder, is it your cowardice
Or theirs that keeps them powerless

You blend in then one day look up
And find you're no longer blending
You discover yourself defending
Those who couldn't pull it off

Or never wanted to...

    Are you the coward after all?

But, what is practical is tactical
    After all
And while the jury is free and living
You were only trying to survive
    After all
And, a necessary evil
Either isn't necessary or isn't evil
    After all
        After all

    Am I the coward after all?

Billy D. Thomas | Mending The Broken

mending The Broken
life I am choking
and Filled with
meds
Hand of Hope,
now open
is The Capital life

mending The Broken
I Have overcome.
of Darkness is
without The meds
my scars shine
my Art and
my cry For Help

mending The Broken
was Taken my life
pained Filled
ness I Killed
Healed Free of

Now in my new life
Joy and Love

my Dark
Deflowered
mind-altering
crying out For a
my eyes are
all I can see
now Bounding me.

The meds
The veil
No more
still Deflowered
Deep. Through
Newfound Friends
is now Being Heard.

my Love
Shaken with
my Heart in sick-
Yet now I am
CPS pills.

I know
Family and Friends.

H. Lee | Our World

Another war threatens the East
Covid runs rampant on all the rest
Things are certainly not at their best
Once again, humans put the world to test
It makes one wonder, it's our behest
Will we survive this new quest
Or, will be laid to rest?
Our world, our lives, are a mess!
Every day it's on the news
Someone who claims to have paid their dues.
So out of their mouth it spews
A pumped-up version of their views
With facts they manage to misconstrue
Particles of truth, so very few
It's the same old, same old, nothing new
Disaster, death, and bullets flew
Stay inside till someone restores order
Many choose to just flee
Becoming another refugee
Out of the pan, into a new fire
Peace and freedom the only desire
At the crossing it's a quagmire
No one in, no one out, they conspire
To keep us down and confused
Nowhere to go, all refused
Why? Why can't we all live free?
Each human sees life differently
Is this circle of chaos our destiny?
Round and round the world turns endlessly

Mark Lott | A World That's Free

At one point we lived
In a world that was free,
Now we live in a world with war,
Hate, racism, and poverty.
People took to killing, hatred, racism
And homophobic attitudes
Instead of accepting each other
With solidarity and gratitude.
A step in the wrong
Direction and way of life,
Leading to stress, struggle,
Pain, and strife.
When the most
Important thing alone,
Is coming together
As one.
To reorganize our world
To a better place,
So each of us through
Victory can replace.
A point in life where
We all agree,
To live in
A world that's free.

Scary Movie | Hourglass

The hourglass
              Drifting

                          Sifting

                                      Falling

                                                Is not the past
                                       But the future forgotten

                                                Is not the present
                                 But memories we get lost in

Each grain

          But a breath

                    A heartbeat

                          Of lives already spent.

Afterword

It has been an honor and a pleasure to edit this poetry anthology, a first for A.B.O. Comix publications. I think what I love most about *"ignite the stars"* is that it exists due to pure happenstance. When I first encountered our full-to-bursting file of poetry collected over the five-year lifespan of A.B.O. Comix, I was rooting through our filing cabinet for something completely different. I asked Casper what the mystery manila folder was all about, and the result is this book. It's truly the little project that could.

I have enjoyed every moment of this undertaking, digging through our archive to find just the right poems and themes to string together into an anthology - and then receiving letters full of fresh new verses that took the whole thing in a different direction. I'm thankful for Casper's unending support on my first big boy book project, and for our incarcerated contributors' trust in sending us these intimate, eloquent expressions of their inner lives. I am indebted to Michael Eaton, Pariah, H. Lee, Billy D. Thomas, Fuller, and Lil Cee Cee, whose words serve as section titles and the title of this book. Thank you for your brilliance; you are all stars.

This will hopefully be the first of many editions of *A Queer Prisoner's Poetry Anthology*. To all of our contributors whose work was not chosen this time around: please keep writing, and keep an eye out for your poems in future anthologies! Your words buoy me, challenge me, move me to tears and help me imagine the more just and beautiful worlds you describe. And if you're reading this from prison and you'd like to try your hand at writing a poem, get in touch:

    A.B.O. Comix c/o Poetry Anthology
    P.O. Box 11584
    195 41st St
    Oakland, CA 94611

- Ollie Mills

How to Help

Thank for reading this collection of poems by incarcerated queer and trans writers. We hope they have inspired you to take action on behalf of these poets to work towards a kinder, more compassionate world.

If you believe in our mission, you can help support us by:

Donating or providing resources:
paypal.me/abocomix | Venmo @abocomix
patreon.com/abocomix | Cashapp: $abocomix

Spreading the word and following us for udpates:
Twitter: @AboComix
Instagram: @a.b.o.comix
Facebook: ABO Comix

Volunteering with us or hosting a fundraising event: email **abocomix@gmail.com** if you're interested!

Writing to someone on the inside:
Check out **www.abocomix.com/bios** to get connected!

Talking to friends, family, neighbors, and community members. Open up a dialogue and remember to meet people where they're at. Don't be afraid of difficult conversations and do your best to maintain an open mind. You may learn something as well. When we know better, we can do better.

Starting your own creative project! Against all odds, we're still here. Still creating, still building friendships, still optimistic about what we can achieve when we work together. Take a chance, work hard and you will do amazing things. Trust us, we've been there.

Love and solidarity always!

www.ingramcontent.com/pod-product-compliance
Lightning Source LLC
Chambersburg PA
CBHW072209100526
44589CB00015B/2440